CONTENTS

1 Invitation to The Still 7

2 Welcome Home 17

3 Open the Door and Enter In 31

4 The Noise Outside of Us 51

5 The Persistent Interior Noise 69

6 The Surrounding Silence 83

7 Getting Lost Once Again 107

8 The Journey's, a New Beginning 119

ACKNOWLEDGEMENTS

I am humbled and honored by the beauty and grace of the women I have had the privilege to journey with over these few years. They have been my *Still* ladies as we stepped together into a world we are just beginning to know.

You are precious.

Cynthia Bell, RN, BSN, Spiritual Director, Miami FL resident; full time advocate for people without opportunities, exposure and support; wife, mother and grandmother. "I weave silence, peace and stillness with a dose of humor and tears into a life of busyness, noise, and interrupters."

Monica Bruning, PhD., PMP, Fish Lake, MN resident; College Faculty Administrator and Consultant; wife and mother. "I am a student of higher education, a senior fitness wannabe, and a fun seeker."

Sara Livingston Floerke, M. Edu., Duluth, MN resident; wife and mother of five. "I spend my days playing hide and seek, looking for my keys, my purse, peace, and my phone."

Kathy Kelly, RN, BSN, Spiritual Director, Duluth, MN resident; lactation consultant, wife, mother and grandmother. "I love to walk along Lake Superior, flower gardening, getting lost in a good book, attending silent retreats, and playing games with my grandchildren."

I applaud the Korte family members for reading, rereading and suffering with my peculiar inconsistencies as I write. Dennis Korte, husband; Denise and L.J. Pagano, daughter and husband; Aaron Korte, son; Danielle Jindra, my granddaughter extraordinaire.

And the instigator of all things possible, David Hazard, my friend first and consultant on all fronts.

INVITATION TO THE STILL

*F*eel the stillness.

An invitation to quiet and calm in a hectic, often senseless, and runaway world. Don't you wish you could accept it?

Step into the stillness.

A thought, a possibility; refreshing, intriguing, elusive.

Be still.

If only . . .

What if it's possible to find not just space for quiet, but something more? A time to catch that deep breath while leaning into a margin of calm? An abiding place for peace that can remain with us even in the middle of life's intense and demanding events?

In our frantic, wearying world, most of us have already found a litany of popular methods for finding calm. These programs most often flag down our time, attention, and money. Stealing those quiet, deep breaths and pulling us away from the calm are smart phones, iPods, Facebook, Twitter, TV commercials, talk shows, and magazines, while the ads are shouting at us to join a gym, shut off those very devices, unfriend, take a walk or a cruise, or take a new drug to ease our stress. Our commercialized world has tapped into our need to pause. Marketers invite us to step into "the Zone" while working hard to pull dollars from the pockets of us "calm-seekers"; "from the boardroom to the playing field and the red carpet" we are looking for "a way to relax, focus and be present."

Truthfully . . .

Do you see yourself adding another item to your daily agenda? Gym membership can be a healthy response, but peace and calm in the midst of the clanking barbells, the throbbing beat of a Zumba class, TV chatter, pumped up adrenalin, and conversation surrounding you—really?

As if the noise existed only outside of us.

Wherever we go, there we are, and the noise never seems to end. We could shut down all our devices, yet the "OFF" button doesn't stop the din of inner voices. The mitigating dramas swirling around our life and our friends' lives take us where we do not want to go again. And ending relationships does not bring peace or solve anything. A walk in the park or the woods is inviting, and yet it can easily turn on you and intensify the inner turmoil. Medicating for stillness too often works in reverse. The bottom line is that the new line of credit you will need to complete the latest calming program just adds to the agitation you are already experiencing.

We get it.

Instinctively, we know that to live well across the spectrum of our mental, physical, emotional, and spiritual lifetime, calmness and serenity enhance our existence. Scientific studies have shown that finding stillness eases bad moods caused by stress and anxiety; sharpens creativity and spontaneity; supports sounder sleep while improving memory; and can reduce the dreaded rising blood pressure. As we move toward stillness, our dimensions of living change. Under the constant clatter and busyness of our lives there is waiting for us a simple, clear space grounded in our source of life.

God.

Surrounded by such noise, agitated to the depths of our being, how do we find the calm we need? How do we connect with the One who is the quiet, steady pulse of our very life?

What is this space and what does it look like?

The artistry of stillness begins with a glance over your shoulder. This brush with memory holds a glimpse of past experience provided by our creator. That instant of quiet is stored within you.

I have moments of such stillness, and I continually add to this bank of stillness as the quiet of God and I connect.

I ask you to travel with me as I move into silence. Pause with me from time to time to take in what you will find. I will tell you of my experience, but it is your experience that will usher you into the *Still*. Even now, in this moment, you may be experiencing anxiety, relief, or energy for the journey. You are on track.

Here is some of what I have found.

While hiking many miles of wilderness in this wonderful country, I have stood before dozens of trailheads. Each one was bursting with possibilities of unknown terrain. I find that as I hike, the mystery draws me in. I anticipate adventure and beauty rarely encountered before. As I leave the parking lot behind, placing one foot in front of the other, the trees and bushes, rocks, and creeks pass by. I am urged on as I climb, nearing breathtaking views, soft breezes ruffling my windbreaker, each encounter calling me to go deeper and take a few more steps around the next bend. Fresh aromas invite me in: pine, balsam, fresh lake water, a field of daisies. I am welcomed and guided to hidden stones, a place to rest. Where the chattering ringtone of my brain had existed, now there is a sense of belonging, quiet, and calm. I stop where I am and sit on a rocky ledge. Thoughts and insights become clearer. In fact, I hadn't realized my life was leading me onto such a dangerous ledge of frantic mindless activity. After a time of insight and introspection, I leave that place. Whether the walk is completed or not, now I know that I will walk with God again.

— pause & reflect —

What instant of stillness do you remember?

What do you recall as bringing the silence to you?

Others have walked before us and have described the stillness in these ways.

Archbishop Desmond Tutu: "Every bit of ground we trample is actually holy ground . . ." "The sacred could erupt anywhere."

Virginia Jarvis: "Going out to the fields on our farm, laying down in the dirt with my ear to the soil and listening."

Henri Nouwen: "A room where Christ can invite us to feast with him at the table of abundance."

Anne LaMott: "A radiance is inside us, just as it is visible outside us; and to seek it is maybe to catch a glimpse from time to time of a light within, of a candle at the window of our heart, of a home somewhere inside."

This book will guide you toward the *Still* that we long for. I want to help you explore the aspects of your disquiet and all the warring factors that stop you from slowing down and flowing into the God-given rhythm of your life.

Allow me to walk with you as we examine that outer wall of noise, chaos, and demands and consider the inner resistance to finding stillness. I want to help you come to view your life from a different perspective.

We will find a slow and simple way to breathe deeply not found at any gym. By unhooking your jammed-up life, you can find that enriching and enlivening sacred space you've been looking for. Don't mistake escape for true inner peace. Your need for this walk can become the courage to begin a journey to live life creatively. The organic rhythm and unity of life preside over the fragmented existence you leave behind. It can all come together as a God-created whole.

"I took time off from work yesterday. I fled to a quiet place and took a walk in the woods. But I couldn't find the stillness in here!" Sandy said as she patted her chest. Physically, mentally, and emotionally spent, she confided that she wanted time for her world to stop whirling. She had come to me for direction. And what she wanted but could not find was a place and time where she could just "be," a little peace to pull herself together.

"I'm so sorry. I get so tired of apologizing for always running late!" Erik mouths this to me, with his phone still up to his ear. Glancing at me, he nods at the phone and rolls his eyes. We agreed to save him time by meeting here at the coffee shop around the corner from his office to talk about finding stillness in his hectic life. "Be still, don't I wish? I can never get away from this," he said, pointing at his phone. "I have four employees counting on me, a wife and two beautiful boys who need my time and attention. Tell me, where does quiet and calm fit into that?"

We know exactly what Sandy and Erik want, don't we? To connect with life again. We've found ourselves lost in a world outside of ourselves amidst the dings and beeps of our devices and the frantic scurry of activity to meet the demands on our time. Part of us is so overstimulated, fueled, and ready for a jet take off that we can't seem to keep our feet on the ground. We yearn for calm, a sanctuary from the current storm, a time for non-rushed, reflective—not reactive—clear thinking. We want an opportunity to stop, slow down, and enter into the keeping, the loving caring activities surrounding us before they are gone. What we want is inner peace, a deep, resounding, natural movement from insanity to refuge, from disruption to homeliness.

But how do we "get to" that quiet space we need?

It's quite simple, actually.

The truth is, we are predisposed to stillness. Stillness is like the breath we draw; it completes the life cycle of our physical body. No need to think about it. It is. It is an involuntary movement functioning without our consent. This *Still* is quietly tucked away in us. The *Still*, the rest, the silence of God dwells in the core of our being. It naturally calls from within, urging us to come and exist for a moment. The source of all light, life, and love, the *Still* is God within us. Together we will rediscover this still place in our hearts.

Sandy was looking for it. Erik knew intuitively that it must be somewhere nearby. Sandy didn't find the *Still* on that walk in the woods, but that was the beginning chapter of her growing toward stillness. For Erik, just making an appointment with someone to talk about being still was a first step in a lifetime journey in the art of living deeply.

I want you to know that this is not a book offering you *x* amount of "steps." The fact is, there are many paths inward to the *Still*. My journey is different from yours. Like Erik, you may approach it exhausted and in a hurry. We are all different and afraid to try something new. We're questioning, curious, and reluctant, maybe unsure. You may even be saying "been there, done that." You may be a bit skeptical or ready to jump in fully.

Where are you at this moment?

Jumpy!

In a cartoon by Bill Watterson, the tiger Hobbes turns to his wild child buddy, Calvin, and says happily, "When you're confronted with the stillness of nature, you can even hear yourself think." Calvin replies, "This is making me nervous. Let's go in."

This simple cartoon acknowledges something else about our desire for stillness: We can want it and not want it at the same time. Stepping into the *Still* has never been easy, even for those who choose to do it.

As soon as we think about seeking stillness, the noise of life gets louder.

The first thing we do is recognize the sounds and sights and thoughts that bar us from entering the *Still*. Whether these noises are outer or inner to our life, we intimately know them. Many noises we entertain are tedious, repetitive, invasive, unannounced, and unwanted, and they keep us preoccupied. We get stuck in their loops and remain overwhelmed, swirling in all the drama. Let's call them out for what they are: engulfing avalanches that obstruct our way to peace and calm.

The way inward will lead us to regions of our lives that require change, release, surrender, and unlearning. On this path to the *Still*, we are pilgrims discovering, claiming, and settling a territory that is ours by birthright. We are no longer tourists in the land of noise as we seek refuge from the controlling, never-ending noise that tries to capture our full attention. We are walking toward a place of serenity in the midst of chaos, calmness while the world keeps exploding, and a silence that exists apart from the world's overbearing beat.

This is what we seek. And our faith promises us, "We will be unshakable and assured and deeply at peace." (John 16:33)

WELCOME HOME

Life's experiences offer us a priceless tapestry of concepts and language, defining and clarifying a pathway to home. They permeate our interior spaces and feed our hunger for the *Still*. I'm about to introduce you to words and pictures used by spiritual mentors, those who have traveled before us and even our contemporaries to find the space we seek. Their words set the stage for us this day. These words are, in fact, the stepping stones to our desire for an agenda-less and safe place to rest for a moment.

Approaching home isn't the same for each of us. When we search for a place where we can be real, find rest, receive love, and have a moment of instant stillness, home comes to mind for some of us, but for others, not so much.

This place is not up, down, or "out there"; it is here within ourselves. It is the place of life within us and has been carried by our faith over the centuries. Ancient believers wrestled and named it, men and women throughout history embraced the search and found a name for it, and by opening the pages of scripture we can hear the words for it offered by the Master.

In this moment we are invited to join the stillness and richness of God's dwelling place.

And yet . . .

Welcome . . .

Home . . .

If the hair on the back of your neck is tingling at the mention of a welcoming home, this would be a souvenir from your past. The words "welcome" and "home" are not an idea we can embrace. Our resistance often comes from a sense of quick anger or guilt from difficult situations we encountered in our childhood family. We have been robbed of the meaning of home as a safe and warm place to be.

I grew up in a home with a mother with out-of-control anger issues. She was a screamer. I know about wanting to live where warmth and love are put forward first. As a child I would catch glimpses of families laughing, having fun together through the windows of houses as we drove by. I wished I lived there. In my childhood and at my house I learned to stay out of the way, tiptoe around, hide, and blame myself for parental shortcomings.

The houses where some of us lived were breeding places for hiding the truth about ourselves and for trying to earn the scraps of love that seemed always to be beyond our reach. We left that home on poor terms years ago. And even recently, when asked, we found we had no time to help with the latest family crisis. The concept of home for us grew into a complicated and duplicating sense of uncaring with superficial responses and deep disappointments.

We haven't all experienced the same, this disgust or love and respect for home. This is one of the very reasons we travel together. We can find encouragement and hope at our side as we walk with others and with the masters of our faith. We are on our way to finding the place we yearn for, to find the *Still*, a home provided by our God.

"God, it seems you've been our home forever, long before the mountains were born, long before you brought earth itself to birth, from 'once upon a time' to 'kingdom come' you are God." (Psalm 90:2)

"Glad to see you" and "you are wanted here" are what each of us seek no matter what our upbringing. The longing for warmth, love, and being ourselves, whispered in hope, is the answer we have been searching for. We yearn for homecoming.

—pause & reflect—

Take a moment and explore your
relationship with "home."
Is it one of hope or discouragement?

Keeping that sense of eagerness
and desire in mind, let's look at how others
have named the place of homecoming.

THE WAY IT IS

The words that follow both highlight and shed light on the shadows of our personal experience of "home." Here are some words and stories to encourage us as we search for meaning.

...solitude, quiet, enter the rest, peace of mind, silent heart...
"From struggle to joy, a seed reveals solitude and quiet."

THE ART OF LIVING DEEPLY

> As I watch my small garden grow from seed to the presentation of a flower or a bean on the stem, I take in the struggle and joy. The seed is buried in the silent earth, the *Still*, and, moving through hardship and happiness, that seed rises with energy and effort bursting out of the earth. The focus, confidence, and solitude it reveals as it shows its fruit is my firsthand picture of the journey to the *Still*. In this fruit I recognize the trek those seeds have made to present me with petunias and sprigs of parsley. It captures for me a bit of this stillness for which I long. —Sara Floerke

. . .stillness, silence of creation, nature, sunrise, sunset . . .
"Stillness in the eye of the hurricane." Cindy Bell

> Coming from a family with five brothers and sisters and growing up on a large farm in the foothills of the Adirondacks, I often sought time for myself. One cool summer day, I wandered down to the creek and lay across the culvert, staring into the water. I lost time watching the water bubble and curve over the stones twisting and turning on its path. There was this inner hush, and I was totally absorbed in that brief moment of quiet, presence, still. The sounds reverberated over me: the breeze; the singing of the birds; the bubbling of the water. —Cindy Bell

" . . . that resting place where we remove ourselves from the demands of our life and allow God to speak in an unhurried manner." Jane Rubietta

"Solace in the woods." Monica Bruning

. . .homeward call, the "yes" to God, the deep rest, peace . . .

"God is our homeland, communion with God in the silence of our heart." Martin Laird

"Homecoming." Henry Nouwen

...Sabbath, inmost self, deep living, whisper...

"A whisper of hope." Kathy Kelly

> "Stillness"
>
> Breath of heaven
>
> Stirring my soul
>
> Arms of embrace
>
> Whisper of hope
>
> Silence
>
> —Kathy Kelley

"That place at the very center of our being that is known by God, that is grounded in God and is one with God." Ruth Haley Barton

...knowing God, prayer, the deep well...

"A dwelling place for the Lord, a warm, well-hollowed, hospitable place where the life of my God will deepen and mature me." Joyce Rupp

...the Still... Tina Korte

—pause & reflect—

As you read and turn these phrases over in your mind, did you find one that resonates in your heart?

THE WAY IT WAS

Tracking the way to the *Still* leads us to those who have gone before us, the ancients. These stalwart men and women of the desert, these mothers and fathers of the faith, recorded their steps for us, just as we have found our own words to describe this path. They left behind these precious words for us. Their longing for the presence of reaches out over time, and they become a part of our lifeline to guide us home. As we come to value our past as making the present possible, we come to understand how close and at what a distance the *Still* remains.

. . .*rest* . . .

"My heart rests in you." David the Psalmist

. . .*home, holy hill* . . .

"A home within the soul." St. Francis of Assisi

...flight, sublime...

"A humble flight from the world." Brigitta of Sweden

...mist, castle, interior dwelling place, sublime dignity, great beauty...

"We begin to see, as through a mist, the first dim outlines of the castle He longs to reveal within us, an interior dwelling place of sublime dignity and great beauty." Teresa of Avila

...roads, good way, heavenly kingdom is near, tabernacle...

"Jeremiah declared, stand by the roads and look and ask for the ancient paths where the good way is and walk in it. Because the heavenly kingdom is found along these ways, not without good reason . . . . The kingdom of heaven is near. So do you want the kingdom of heaven to also be near for you?" Chromatious of Aquileia

What comes to mind for you as you read these ancient meanings for home? Go back over these words, reading them and circling the ones that tell you of a space where stillness and love are available for you.

THE WAY OF PAST AND PRESENT IN SCRIPTURE

Finding our way home employs yet a deeper language, a language of love and of belonging. We learn to listen again in a new way. Those who walked and talked with the man of peace, Jesus, found their way hearing the language of stillness directly from him. He had sought them out to give them their lives back. These are the words that give us yet a deeper entrance to the *Still*.

...*the way*...

"Keep your eyes on the one who knows the way." (John 14:6–7)

...*living, water*...

"rivers of living water," (John 7:38)

"given you living water." (John 4:10)

"a spring of water welling up" (John 4:14)

...*light, life*...

"light of life . . ." (John 8:12)

...*free*...

"You will be free indeed." (John 8:37)

...*pasture*...

"Go in and go out and find pasture." (John 10:9)

...*peace*...

"Peace, I leave with you, my peace I give to you." (John 14:27)

"Peace, be still." (Mark 4:35–41)

... *home* ...

"Today is the day I will be a guest in your home." (Luke 19:5)

— pause & reflect —

These words and phrases
from scripture mean welcome
and homecoming in our lives today
as much as they have for
our ancestors.

Have you heard these words before?

Which one(s) invite you in?

Just as the trailheads of each hike draw me into a deepening experience and move me closer to the *Still*, as I read again these words, I encounter that same desire to enter in.

We may have lots of words or no words, pictures or a blank page, a resting place or a whispered silence. It doesn't matter, we are aware of the *Still* coming near. It is for this reason that you and I are taking this *Still* journey together. We are learning from one another through description the depth and richness of God's place for us in his great love. This is our standing invitation to come as we are.

Welcome home.

— pause & reflect —

How would you describe
for yourself home, the peace, the *Still*,
you have been searching for?

What are your words for the place,
the Still, where you yearn to be?

A CALL TO COME AWAY
AND WALK . . . FOR A MOMENT . . .

Find a quiet spot, a stool at your kitchen bar, out on the grassy lawn, or even the bathroom at work.

Sit by yourself and come away in your heart.

Place you hand on something solid—a wall, a desk, or tree near you.

Breathe in . . .

The space you are in . . .

Breathe it in . . .

In this moment . . . listen, smell, see, touch, and taste.

All of that is you and it is present . . .

Breathe out . . .

Let go of work or the family or tasks that need to get done . . .

Be aware of this space . . .

Breathe in . . . Breathe out . . .

Welcome Home!

OPEN THE DOOR AND ENTER IN

We don't choose the ringtone that summons us to enter the *Still,* the one that invites us to the deep core of our being. That longing comes from a felt need arising from the sight of a sunrise, from suffering a broken heart, or from an inner sense of desperation and fear. The call to enter a place of rest comes with great joy or a need for comfort and help.

To enter the *Still* so you can find a whisper in the middle of a storm is as simple or as difficult as stepping from one room to another. Place your hand on the knob, turn it, and step across the threshold. Remain yourself, ordinary and authentic. Embrace with delight the moment that ushers you into a great mystery!

How we do it, with hesitation or speed, questioning or decisively, is what we discover as we move forward. Our individual way is before us. We can't predict what we'll find. Fast or slow, high or low, and everything in between will be distinctly you. The adventure awaits.

"Keep your eyes on the one who knows the way to take you where you need to go." (John 14:6–9)

THRESHOLD

Hold on to the doorknob and open the door. We are stepping into the *Still,* a space for ourselves and God to exist. We inhale fresh air. We take deep breaths. The reality of what we are to be and do will be revealed as we dwell. Remember, we have come to step out of our ongoing routine and find a different path to stillness and peace.

"The Lord is near." (Philippians 4:5)

With our first step, we leave behind the pressures, the to-do lists, the expectations, and the need to have things exactly the way we want them. The *Still* is not all about us. This experience in the *Still* is not about accomplishing, gaining, or enforcing our positions. In fact, when we find this place, we are released from pleading, convincing, and presenting our will.

> **STILLNESS AS A YOUNG MOTHER**
>
> Finding the quiet and stillness as a young mother certainly had its own set of challenges. With young children and babies in my care, it was difficult to carve out time to be still for myself. When I had two children in school and two at home and I finally got the older ones out the door and on the bus, I would go back to bed. Not to sleep but to sit with my Bible on my bed tray and enjoy as much time with God as I could. My littlest boys would play in their room next to mine, often interrupting for one reason or another. After some frustration, I decided it was good for them to see their mother spending time with God, even if they had to wait a few minutes for their needs to be met. —Kathy Kelley

I experience a full range of emotions and thoughts as I enter the *Still*. Recently I felt beaten up by an overwhelming world around me. My husband and I had left our home of twenty-five years in Duluth, Minnesota. We have moved many times in our life, but this time it had been two years since we had a place to call home.

I had come to a place where I felt I was dangling in the air. This is how I expressed it one morning in the middle of that disturbance.

All around me, such sweet stillness.
I exist in full color.
Noise crashing in, shattering the silence.
a tree falls, another and another,
another house to see, another bid to make,
my body weary, a season filled with chiggers,
yes, chiggers,
no heat, broken appliances,
sickness in the family, a cough breaks in the night,
family on the edge, bewildering, quiet,
no sleep for Dennis, he shakes,
can't shake off a body out of control,
All challenging the calm.
Tears well up, spilling over.
My body lets go.
The Still returns around me.
I exist.

The path we take to the *Still* differs for each of us and changes as we find our way. There is no "right" way to enter in.

What follows is a broad sweep of what happens as we enter into in the *Still*, in no particular order.

COME AS YOU ARE

As we set foot into the *Still* for the first time, we may enter as a stranger, a guest, or perhaps as a child. In time, we enter as a member of the family.

"While he was yet a long way off . . ." (Luke 15:11–32)

With this phrase the premier scripture story for hospitality begins. Jesus told it for anyone who would listen. This home, the *Still*, has a seasoned host, with a documented and well-rehearsed welcome. God invites us to step into a loving embrace.

As we open the door, we recognize that our homecoming has been hoped for, planned for, and is a matter of great joy for our host. Our welcome is a big deal. Please take it personally!

As we step across the threshold, we come as we are. No need to dress in a uniform of beliefs or put on a false face or crawl in on our knees. We are coming to our soul's true home.

At one point, I decided that what I was responding to in the morning as I entered the *Still* was the coffee, not God. So I cut coffee out of my life. I reasoned that if my devotion to God is real, I'm not going to let this coffee get in the way! I don't remember what my quiet times were like without the coffee, but I discovered that if I don't drink coffee I have absolutely no personality. It's not that I was just tired. I was a complete blah. Going without coffee wasn't worth going without a personality. This is where grace comes in. God made coffee. God made me. I'm not ashamed that coffee has become as integral to my spirituality routine as my Bible. Coffee doesn't speak to me like the Bible, coffee doesn't illuminate like prayer, coffee doesn't whisper to me like a meditation. Coffee, like the rocker I sit in or the afghan I throw over my shoulders, is a vehicle to help me be alert and ready my heart and mind. —Sara Floerke

A wonderful possibility emerges as we set foot into the *Still*. We have found a time and place to be ourselves. The wow of just being who we are with the assurance we are loved begins to exist. This is the peace we have longed for. Our forward movement is to make ourselves at home.

This feeling of welcome comes from within ourselves; no other can present us with that reality. The welcome is found by breathing it in, living it, and accepting it. Truth and knowing love occur over time, unfolding in God's time.

— pause & reflect —

How do you enter the *Still*? As a stranger, a guest, or a member of the family?

How long does it take to be yourself?

IN THIS MOMENT

If it beeps or buzzes, our focus follows that sound to another world, time, and place. It is possible to travel mentally from here to Timbuktu and back in a second while our feet remain planted where we are. But it is in this moment, this place, here and now, fully present that we exist within the stillness of God.

Where is here and now?

Breathing and feeling our lungs draw in and push out situates us in the here and now. Recognizing that our life is fully in God's hands and resting in the knowing is living the *Still*.

> **BELLY BREATHING, THE MARTIAL ART OF THE *STILL*:** Breathing: We take it for granted. When the doctor asks us to "take a deep breath" and she puts the stethoscope to our chest, we instinctively expand our chest and raise our shoulders in an effort to draw in a deep breath. This type of breathing is inefficient for the *Still*. Watch a newborn breathe. Their little bellies rise up and down. They are breathing from their diaphragm. Babies are belly breathing. Then, as we grow up, we forget how to belly breathe. We become shallow breathers. We only expand our chests, not allowing for deeper, cleansing breath.

> To assess your breathing, lie on your back and place one hand on your belly and the other on your chest. As you inhale, push your belly out as far as possible. Does your hand rise on your belly while the hand on your chest does not? Now, as you exhale, does your hand on your belly fall toward the floor? This type of breathing will nourish your body, mind, and spirit. Embrace the baby's breath daily. It will become natural, simple, and ordinary in your life. Inhale, hold, exhale, repeat. Do this three to five times as you begin your time in the *Still*. —Aaron Korte, RN, RCEP, CDE

God is in the *Still*—the place where clock time is suspended. Staying in the here and now is intentional. Simple this is not. We gain entrance with new eyes and ears, childlike. What is in this exact moment that is so special? Today, this hour, minute, and second is where we learn to respond to our life in real time. Being present, focusing on this moment, is where we want to be.

We take tentative steps at first. As we grow bolder, we find we use a different type of energy. We are connected with the strength of the centuries. We join those who courageously forged their path before us. We don't know the lives they lived, but we draw upon their fearless heart and accompany them as we walk the same direction.

God is here, constant and consistent. He will always be here, faithful and promising never to leave us.

God is now. God is present.

—pause & reflect—

How's your breathing?

Do you have time to belly breathe?

What difference would this make in your life?

Where are you here and now, this moment?

MOVEMENT

As we step across the threshold, we do not enter a museum filled with dead artifacts, nor is this a placid sea going nowhere. The *Still* is a living, growing existence. We are no longer doing

God—we are being with God. This is our real home. And like any home you move into, there is a period of adjustment.

Stops and starts are to be expected, and we adjust as we go along. Staying fluid develops over time, with help from our Creator. We will find tried and true ancient paths and brief walkways. We will follow, unfortunately, some sidetracks and alleys. Popular highways will get our attention. And we may even take a tollway or two, costing us a little cash. These parts of our journey are yet to be experienced. Or perhaps you have already trekked around the periphery of some of these places.

We live on the edge of movement in the present, and we move and change as we settle in. There will be times when we feel as if we take two steps forward only to find we have made three steps backward. We get up, step forward, and breathe deep. We repeat that process time and again. Then, there are times, even the next day, we find no stillness. We may find the peace and the rest has gone missing.

At such a moment in my life I made this primary discovery: We don't go backward in the *Still*. Going through a rough spell at an edgy time of my life, I felt, not only stalled out, but going backwards in my *Still* life.

As I reviewed my journey looking for answers, I realized that when I step boldly into the here and now, movement happens. When I began in this *Still* journey I followed what I wanted. I had the kind of peace I thought I should have. I wanted God to be where I had imagined, in a quiet sanctuary waiting for me when I was ready, calm, and collected.

As I came to rely on this quiet and it didn't happen, I interpreted that as going backward. One day as I read scripture, I bumped into John 1:16. It seems I had been given the gift of the *Still*, and I was about to receive another gift on top of that one. I had been receiving freely the gift of peace and self-knowledge. Now I was ready for a grace in place of that grace. New gifts were coming my way.

And they are coming your way too.

In that moment I found myself moving away from what I selfishly wanted. This new stillness leads me toward God's great love on an even more picturesque path. It's just another way to find the *Still*.

Think about that: The peace and calm we have already received in the *Still* are expanding to include a brand-new kind of grace, a fresher deeper grace to replace the old. Finding the *Still* and realizing it isn't always an easy way—this is learning the art of deep living.

"Stillness is what creates Love.

Movement is what creates Life.

To be still, yet still moving, that is everything."
Do Hyun Choe

This is what awaits us in the *Still*.

— pause & reflect —

What adjustments have you encountered
so far as you enter the *Still*?

Have you bumped into a step or two that
created doubt or caused backward movement?
When and how?

PERSONAL FORM OR RITUAL

Entering a dark room and feeling blind is like stepping into the *Still* for the first time. But written on our DNA there is a thread, the blueprint for our personal pathway for calm. The colors we choose, the lump of clay we mold, the notes we hum, create daily the *Still*. It's the form we're shaping in our innermost self to hold the hope of deep rest. The pattern emerging will depend more and more on who we are becoming as our routine unfolds.

What is our routine? What is it we actually do?

We take the next step into the darkness, feeling our way

with one foot in front of the other. By taking that first step, our personal form of ritual has begun. We are already on the move!

My first steps were clumsy. I was hesitant. I was fearful I might offend some of my spiritual colleagues. After all, what I was doing was so simplistic. It did not feel very spiritual!

In real time, I chose a physically soft place to land. I claimed an old and soft comfortable chair. I placed it in a restful spot where I could get a view of outdoors, day or night. As I am an early riser, my time was set. Now I had a time and place, the beginning of a form.

When we first step out sets up the next time we come. We will step in familiarly, doing it in that same manner, because it got us where we wanted to go. And if we didn't get there, we will change up the routine with enthusiasm. We either begin to trust our first pattern or we will need to try another way.

Natural to who we are individually is the way we continue to go. Does that mean we follow a program? Will we find restrictions? Does the path narrow? Are there three easy steps? Will we journey in the footsteps of an ancient saint or mystic?

In time, you will know how it happens for you.

I have heard people denigrating the place of ritual, saying it is a way for people to avoid not thinking through things thoroughly on their own. Although this can be true if we are not mindful and present, I believe ritual has very much to do with allowing the spiritual and emotional side of me to be nourished. As a young person I began having a "quiet time" every morning. Always dutiful and responsible, I simply was responding to the directive of my Sunday School teachers. And years later . . . "I'm not even sure God is real," I heard myself say. I was going through all the doubts and asking questions one has over time. But I couldn't escape that thirty-year routine of seeking the Lord every morning. My body or my spirit or something wouldn't let me rest. So I started getting up early and just sitting, crossing my arms, not seeking God. In the quiet of my room with my coffee I wasn't allowed to

> hide very long. God sought me out and reminded me of all the hours we had spent together, days and months and years of thoughtful and heart-filled experiences. I now look at that quiet routine—that morning ritual—as what saved my faith. I realized that I can't eradicate God from my life. We have spent so much time together that I simply can't be without that time in the *Still*. That's when I realized what a gift the discipline of daily quiet time with God is. —Sara Floerke

—pause & reflect—

At this moment, what is most natural for you?

A program, easy steps, following your heart?

How would you describe your ritual?

How will you proceed?

We each have our own style for approaching a mystery. Any guidelines we find here are only that, not steps to be copied.

If we are looking for a deep voice from the sky or a great crescendo with a grand finale as evidence that we have entered the *Still*, it will not occur when we want it to. It appears after the encounter with growth and time. There are no quick check-off boxes in this process. We are slowly being changed, and encounters add up.

COACHING HELPS

To aid your journey here are a few helps:

1. To get in touch with who you are, look at yourself in a mirror.
   Ask, "Who am I?"
   What is the first thought that comes into your mind?

   You probably noticed the blemish on your forehead, the receding hairline, the need to shave, something to pluck or comb. Focusing on what you already know about yourself usually takes on a life of its own, and you are the loser.
   The focus is on how God sees you.

2. To practice recognizing time:
   Place a timer, watch, phone, or clock next to you. You will be measuring a moment in stillness.
   Start with a minute. Be still, breathe deep, and wait until you think a minute has gone by. Then move on to three minutes, then ten minutes.

3. Belly breathing. Start with three whopping big belly breaths. After the three breaths, sink into that fresh air flowing in your body.

4. Light a candle. Set up your candle and lighter before you begin your breaths. Light it and as you watch the flame, feel the business in your life drift away. Sink into the flame and sense the warmth of letting go.

5. There are as many ways to find the *Still* as there are individuals searching for it. Here are a few of those ways for your investigation: riding a horse, riding a motorcycle, watching a sunrise or a sunset, walking a labyrinth or coloring in a mandala, doing a Lectio Divina, writing a prayer, or any other form that helps you.

SCRIPTURES

"Keep your eyes on the one who knows the way to take you where you need to go." (John 14:6–9 The Message)

"Come away with me by yourselves to a quiet place and get some rest." (Mark 6:31)

"The Lord is near." (Philippians 4:5)

"I knew that you would always hear me." (John 11:42)

". . . Stilled the storm to a whisper." (Psalms 107:29)

A CALL TO COME AWAY AND WALK . . . FOR A MOMENT . . .

Leave behind the beeping and the buzzing.

Take a deep breath.

Place your feet on the ground. Where are they? In your living room, on the porch, or under your seat on a park bench?

This is the here and now.

In your heart, stand at the doorway to the *Still*.

The rest, the peace you have been waiting for is here.

These gifts of grace are being freely offered.

Breathe in.

Allow the one who knows the way to take you where you need to go.

THE NOISE
OUTSIDE OF US

"What the f*** do you want?" Loud cursing, arguing, and doors banging came from somewhere across the lake. The vacationing revelers burst into my quiet space, reverberating across the lake in the early hours.

My plan had been to meet the day with the sounds of the friendly frogs, chirping birds, ruffling wind, and the sunrise on the opposite shore. But the offensive words and ill-tempered arguments rose and fell as the partiers found new fodder to fight about.

When silence came, I breathed in and settled down. Then bam! It was back. I battled between the freshness of awakening, what I wanted, and the noise that grated on me. The shouting match won, so I picked up my cup of coffee, walked away, and shut the back door behind me.

Noise surprises us, drags us out of our comfort zone, and persists in the places where we live. The levels, echoes, hurly-burly pace, stops and starts are a part of our rich lives. From the barking of a dog at the mailman to the personalized ringtone on our phone, there is a quantity of unneeded, unwanted noise in each of our lives.

In this reading we will acknowledge the noise outside of us, define it, consider the mischief and harm it plays on our time and health, and call it by name. On our way to the *Still,* we will examine that outer wall of noise, the chaos, and its demand on our focus.

THE MISCHIEF AND HARM OF NOISE

Often, our individual and cultural beliefs about the value of stillness create mischief and can even harm us as we seek the *Still*. Without realizing it, most of us have embraced beliefs that run along these lines: silence is death; noise keeps us awake to life; the excess issues of everyday life are urgent and need immediate attention. Noise is shrewdly stealing the stillness we need for healthy responses to others and to our own interior challenges.

As a radio host for many years, I respected and felt the prompting when the *On Air* light went on. Silence was a bad thing. Moments of silence are called dead time. Filling any silence with banter, facts, anything that keeps the audience engaged was absolutely necessary. This belief invading our lives is an artificial urgency, gobbling up what we want: stillness. It's as if we live with the *On Air* light flashing with airtime to fill.

Our need to feel alive aids that rascal noise. We begin to believe that we come alive by ramping up the frequency and volume anywhere and anytime. Add our overloaded schedules to that legion of sound, and we are kept feeling artificially needed and alive.

Too quiet—*boring!* Take a little time to be at peace—*boring!* In our world, the underlying belief is that peace and serenity are equal to boredom.

"Boredom is the root of all evil, the despairing refusal to be oneself." Soren Kierkegaard

When noise data is gathered, we learn quickly that electronics and social media are taking away our time. Silence is being stolen at an alarming rate. As consumers of noise, we at the least, spend 974 hours of the year listening to the radio; 1,555 hours watching TV; 86 hours playing video games; 195

hours using the internet. There are more TVs than people. We let ourselves be bombarded with sound.

All of this surround sound with so little meaning robs us of precious time, and the effects of too much noise rob us of wellness. Fatigue, stress, sleep problems, trouble concentrating, memory problems, depression, anxiety, and irritability are a few of the physical maladies associated with unwanted sound or noise pollution.

Boredom and urgency have become bedfellows. We are either weary with the monotony of life or dealing with excessive pressing matters: the news, the weather, the safety of our environment. The list of people and issues demanding our immediate attention goes on, and we fear the price to be paid if we are not attentive.

Noise can be addictive. It can become habitual and obsessive. If it threatens to dissipate, we automatically look for it in other places. As our noise runs low, we simply attach ourselves to the noises of others. Noise is available to all of us on social media, reality TV, or, as it always has been, a phone call or cup of coffee away. Others' dramas become personal. We unknowingly pick them up and carry them with us.

As a stay-at-home mom, I was hooked on a soap opera that came on at noon, *As the World Turns*. I fed my kids lunch early and put them down for their naps. This was my signal that this exciting world of conflict and revenge could enter my world. I sat on the edge of my seat as I ate my lunch. I would get angry, weep, and laugh at impossible situations. No rest or time for myself to sew or write, and God help those kids if they interrupted this made-up world. These characters had become intimate friends and deserved my full attention. (Confession: Now I don't watch soap operas or continuing series, but I still grab my lunch and turn on the TV to watch the noon news or HGTV.)

Finally, there is a chain reaction. One noise clings to several others, like the unraveling of a thread or a falling house of cards. The dog barks and we listen for someone at the door or in the driveway. Hearing no one, we finally get up to see what's going on. We see a dirty dish on the counter. Who left it there? We conjure up a scenario of the culprit and an ongoing conflict with the guilty party, complete with words and blame. We see or hear or smell or touch one noise and then several come together, piling up in our head and heart, effectively calling to a halt our way to the *Still*.

If we believe, even in a small way, that silence is death and serenity is boring and that noise is a source of life and all the issues of life are urgent and need immediate attention, then noise is winning, even as we attempt to journey to the *Still*.

— pause & reflect —

Are you ever bored?

What do you do when bored?

How many hours is your TV turned on?
Your video games?

Do you vacillate between
boredom and urgency?

When was the last time someone
else's drama invaded your life?

Who was it: a friend, a TV series, a breaking news story, or an urgent weather report?

Our journey to the *Still* requires of us the review of the noise that never stops. Let's begin by defining noise.

DEFINITION

What would you call noise? To name what is noise in our lives, we need to find our own definition, the types of noises we get hung up on. Here are definitions from experts and individuals like us:

"Loud, confused or senseless shouting or outcry." Webster

"Unwanted sound." OSHA (Occupational Safety Health Administration)

"A pollutant." Les Blomberg

"Sound out of place." G.W.C. Kaye

"Anything that interrupts a signal." Jamie Kassler

"Living in the chaotic outer bands of the hurricane." Cindy Bell

"Chaos and insecurity." Monica Bruning

"Cacophony in my soul." Kathy Kelly

"Anything that gets between me and keeping company with God." Tina Korte

— pause & reflect —

Identify a noise(s) that has occurred recently. What would be your definition of that noise?

TYPES OF NOISES

As a teacher of communication for married couples, I found a very simple way to type noises and stay in the here and now. The present is extremely important on our journey to the *Still*. By using our physical sensations, we can identify and sharpen the when and where and how we are. Noise most often starts with the obvious, hearing or *ear noise*. What we see can stop us in our tracks, *eye noise*. A smell, stinky or fragrant, can force us to abandon ship, *nose noise*. Thoughts about something delicious, like a cinnamon roll with melting butter, can take us to another time and place, *taste noise*. And the sensation of gentle hands or a cold breeze steers my moment into another world, *touch noise*. The world of noise from our senses' perspective is crowded. It's a wonder we find our way through that minefield.

— pause & reflect —

In the moment you have now, pause and account for the sounds and noises surrounding you.

What do you
. . . hear?
. . . see?
. . . smell?
. . . taste?
. . . feel?

Are these noises good or bad?

Early one morning as I shuffled into the kitchen, expecting the sweet aroma of coffee, it wasn't coffee I smelled. Following that odor, I found myself face-to-face with the source, a mess left by our dog around my desk in the office. During the night our dog, Pikku, had been sick. I cleaned it up and returned and picked up where I left off, my quiet time with coffee in hand to be still. It wasn't the task of cleaning up that claimed my stillness. It was the awful odor clinging to my nostrils that invaded the *Still*.

> I work with students who have disabilities and have discovered that when students have sensory disorders, it means their senses don't work properly. These are the students who can't think, because they can feel the seams inside their socks at all times, because the sound of the person breathing beside them is too loud, because the flash of the sun on the leaves is distracting, because the aftertaste of the chicken patties at lunch is strong, because

> the smell of the disinfectant on the desk is overpowering. These are kids who can't work on learning because their other senses don't know how to shut down. These students are a magnification of what many of us face daily. Even if you were to stand totally still, there would be so much noise going on that it is almost impossible to find the one thing, the one voice which is essential, God's voice. The *Still* is what happens when all of that clamoring can shut down enough to distill your life to the most basic essence of being. —Sara Floerke

TIMES AND PLACES . . . AND NOISES

We have within our reach times and places when and where stillness is not available. Even as I mention this you probably have identified a workplace, a family time, or noisy times and places that are labeled for sound. It's good to find this out before identifying where stillness might be found.

— pause & reflect —

Where do I find the loudest and quietest places?

When do they occur? Time of day or season.

Who or what is at the top of my list for demanding that I listen?

OSHA has spent millions of dollars on studying noise pollution in depth, and the results have produced realistic ways of identifying trouble spots. For our benefit, I suggest we use several of their methods to give us a broad look at this noise problem in our life.

NOISE MAPS AND CODES

While mapping and coding noise pollution in the United States, OSHA has located the parts of the country that reflect the loudest, most deafening noise, including airports, highways, and even office buildings. OSHA uses a specific code to measure and restrict the amount of disturbances a certain noise can make.

In our search for quality control in our personal lives, we want to discover where and when noises occur. We can't use their systems, but we can map out our week, where we go, and who we see and track these outer noises where we live, work, and travel.

As we review our loudest noises, we will find that we have already developed a code of our own. In place and created by us for self-preservation. It hasn't given us the stillness we need, or we wouldn't be reading this book. By using the complete set of noises, including sight, smell, taste, touch, and hearing, we can discover how we have done just that—created a code. Here's some of what I found.

- » I am allergic to certain odors, so I avoid cosmetic counters and fabric stores.
- » I use unscented detergents and moisturizers.
- » I keep the clutter in my house to a minimum.
- » Much to my husband's chagrin, I like it quiet in the car when I drive.
- » I don't like the feel of greasy foods in my mouth, so I avoid them.
- » I get up and leave the room if a speaker, teacher, or preacher is yelling or screaming.
- » I asked my children to use "indoor voices" as they enter the house.

There are more things such as noisy crowds, appliances, dogs, and neighbors that I continually re-evaluate. I do this not to eliminate them but to mediate for my peace of mind.

— pause & reflect —

Think of your daily life as a map.
Walk through each day of the week and
circle in your mind or write down
the noisiest places in a typical week.

Using all your senses.
What noises do you restrict or permit?

Where and what time of day
do the loudest noises occur?

How do you regulate TV and computer time
for you or your family?

What is in place already to guard you
from the noises you find hard to handle?

What is the first noise of your day,
and what could you change?

NAMING OUR OUTER NOISES

Let's turn now to naming our designated outer noises—the ones we own. Anything that has a claim on us and takes away the stillness needs to be tagged. What hinders my journey is likely to be different from yours. There isn't an existing noise that doesn't land in some way on someone's unwanted list.

"You cannot keep birds from flying over your head, but you can keep them from building a nest in your hair." Martin Luther

Outer noises are generated by outside forces. Often audible and adjustable, they are easiest to identify. If only we could turn them off by pushing a button, flipping a switch, or closing a door. Look at the partial list below and take note of what makes the most noise on your way to the *Still*.

blender/appliances   traffic   holidays   health
social media   tasks around food   household chores
technology   TV   clutter   stuff   lawnmower
shopping   newspaper   phone   pets   weather conditions
relationships/children   networking   multitasking
friends/coworkers

— pause & reflect —

Circle those above that slow down
your journey, or make a list.

What do you consider outer noise
in your life as you move through your day?

Add what is missing.

> Pain and brokenness can be very noisy
>
> Screaming for attention
>
> Paralyzing my body, mind, and soul
>
> I am reminded of all those
>
> Who suffer in this world
>
> And become one with them. —Kathy Kelley

As I look at the outer noises that stop me, time and time again I find that multitasking is top of my list. Multitasking, a big business rage a few years ago, was touted as the latest trend in staying ahead of the work force. I gravitated toward it because I have a genuine desire to get things done quickly. However,

I found as time went on with so much on my plate, I started to falter. I lost my footing when my brain was forced to do too many things at one time.

I recently read in a Mayo Clinic Health newsletter that multitasking was something we train our brain to do. As we rapidly switch back and forth from one task to another, it is difficult to retain complete information on many fronts at the same time. I realized I did this to myself. I have trained my mind to be distracted on many fronts at the same time.

Now that we have reviewed the outer noises, let's turn to our inner noises.

A CALL TO COME AWAY AND WALK FOR A MOMENT . . .

Breathe in . . .

Breathe out . . .

Noise . . .

Listen . . .

What do you hear?

Clock ticking . . . street sounds . . . voices somewhere?

Breathe in . . .

Breathe out . . .

What are you seeing?

Look around.

Words on this page . . . a wall . . . a chair . . . trees . . . joggers?

Breathe in . . .

Breathe out . . .

Reach out, what do you touch?

This book . . . a pen . . . a container of soda . . . your feet on the ground . . . a desk.

Breathe in . . .

Breathe out . . .

What odors do you detect?

Paper . . . coffee . . . hand sanitizer . . . someone's aftershave lotion.

What are you tasting?

Coffee . . . mint . . . leftover lunch.

Take a deep breath.

Breathe in . . .

Breathe out . . .

You are in this moment.

Welcome to the *Still*.

THE PERSISTENT INTERIOR NOISE

Our interior life has kept psychiatrists and psychologists in business since the nineteenth century. There has never been a culture more aware of the noises that grow inside of us. The mapping and coding of the persona existing inside, dwelling amid our latent memories, our self-protection maneuvers, and our emotional highs and lows, is available online, in a therapist's office, or in a group.

Together we will walk, while treading lightly, into this mysterious place known as the soul.

"For the journey of faith and truth is traveled not with bodily steps but with strides of the interior life." Chromatius of Aquileia

Noises keep us from entering the *Still*. Outer and inner noises differ. The outer noises in our life are just that, outside ourselves but affecting us internally. OSHA's maps and codes can mitigate and help us adjust short-term disturbances. The interior noises hold sway within, while affecting our entire existence long term. OSHA can't map or code the inner life.

If we want to progress on our journey into the sanctuary of peace, strength, and life itself, we need to acknowledge the weight of inner noise, define it, and call it by name. We also need to consider those noises we usually try to avoid. They are buried deep down and have a grip on us. If getting rid of noise was like sweeping a tiled kitchen floor, inner noise would be the dirt and grime that the broom misses because it's stuck in the crevices.

Why do we need to do this kind of inner examination? Because the unsettling noises do not stay hidden deep in the cracks. They regularly make themselves known, *especially* when we are walking towards the *Still*.

Henry Nouwen asks this question: "Is your inner life like a banana tree with monkeys jumping up and down?" He was referring to the worries, fears, and childhood voices jumping up and down whenever we take that deep breath to sit in the here and now. Will they ever stop? What are we harboring that brings our journey to a halt?

You may say, nothing. But let's look:

Are you a worrier, leveling the nap on your living room rug as you pace back and forth?

Have the people you love backed away, as your body tenses up or your expressions or words exhibit a fiery reaction?

Is this one of the mornings when you need to get up for work but your body feels the fall-out of what you ate or drank last night?

Did you stay up all night gaming, avoiding your family and leaving them to fend for themselves?

I get it.

As much as the *Still* is where we'd like to be, sometimes our insides clamor for attention. These are noises we are unable to understand or deal with lightly.

I need to apologize at this point to anyone who feels I am treating their personal pain too lightly. As a counselor, I know how deep these noises go. They have a life of their own. This writing does not take the place of having a good long talk with someone you trust, addressing your past head-on in therapy, or working with a physician if you need pharmaceuticals to calm and quiet your mind temporarily. These needs are very real.

> The inner noise is almost deafening
>
> Myriad voices calling
>
> Like the siren songs
>
> Luring me away from the stillness
>
> Scrambling the signals
>
> Drawing me away from where I want to be
>
> Conversations replayed
>
> Wheels turning
>
> Problem solving
>
> Plans for tomorrow.
>
> —Kathy Kelley

Being hounded by our past and swept backward into good or bad memories and feelings of helplessness robs us of *this* moment. And it is in this silence, if we can part with the past, that we can hear and see the all-encompassing presence of God.

"A loss of silence is as serious as a loss of memory and just as disorienting. Silence is, after all, the natural context from which we listen." Cornelius Plantinga, Jr.

We have the freedom to step into the *Still* just exactly the way we are. And that is the direction in which we are headed.

If anyone is acquainted with noises, I am. This began in my own curious childhood. As I moved along in life, I started—and continue to do—counseling, pastoral counseling, and, finally, spiritual direction. I am very familiar with the inner life and guiding individuals toward the freedom to live in peace.

These noises that interfere with staying in the present might be single and simple. A simple fear is one that keeps us from going down into the basement easily or sleeping soundly at night. Addressing the issue and letting it go may be all it takes.

As worries go, they often grow into complex and complicated phenomenon. It may be that we watched as someone in our childhood home was belittled and made to do things they didn't want to do. Our inner life sucked in a drama to be continued in our relationships. We may have been parented badly and we unknowingly continued that bad parenting. Here are other stories I have heard.

» Deep grief from the tragedy of an early death of a spouse and the pain of miscarriage after miscarriage.

» The loss of a prestigious job and being abruptly pushed and molded into another culture and style of labor.

- » Being lost and searching for family, feeling like an orphan unable to fit in.

- » Getting a divorce in a strict religious and/or family-oriented culture.

- » Being sexually abused in the childhood home, barely surviving attempts to take their own life.

These scenes from our lives are replayed time after time as we hope and search for stillness away from them. We are left clogged up and running as fast as we can. We are stopped before we can find the *Still* or stalled out from the continuing peace the *Still* has already provided us.

IDENTIFYING OUR INTERIOR NOISES

Let us now walk together to the place where we can identify some of the weighted noises, place them in a time frame and perhaps find the trigger that turns them on.

First, let's check back in the outer noise section and review the definition you might have found for noise. Remember these?

"Loud, confused or senseless shouting or outcry." Webster

"Unwanted sound." OSHA (Occupational Safety Health Administration)

"A pollutant." Les Blomberg

"Sound out of place." G.W.C. Kaye

"Anything that interrupts a signal." Jamie Kassler

"Living in the chaotic outer bands of the hurricane." Cindy Bell

"Chaos and insecurity." Monica Bruning

"Cacophony in my soul." Kathy Kelly

My definition for noise is *anything that stops me from keeping company with God.*

I have a lot of interior noises, and some weigh more than others. I find I often will be reminded by my mother's voice how "lazy and messy" I am. If my day has gone south already, which is when I really need the calm and peace, my mother's voice may surface.

Identifying and tracking these interior noises will prove to be deeper and trickier than uncovering those outer ones. Inner noises don't always have a beginning or an end. We find there are no on/off buttons to push. When our hearts and minds team up, we often get taken where we do not want to go.

Think of the types of noises our senses offer—seeing, hearing, tasting, touching, or smelling. These often lead us into the noise we are wanting to avoid. Walking toward the *Still* and hearing a voice from the past or smelling a piece of burnt toast in the present may interfere with being in the here and now, as a memory floods in. The noise of a sense can inadvertently take us away to another time and place as we are trying to focus on the now.

Odors can pull me away from the moment I'm in. The smell of wet wool triggers fear, anxiety, and sadness. On a cold January day in Duluth, Minnesota, I find myself knocking frantically on the front door of my childhood house, trying to get my mother's attention. I was sent outside to play and had lots of fun, but my fingers were beginning to sting and burn and go numb with cold, and I was shivering. I wanted in to warm up. When the door opened, the first thing I did was take off my woolen mittens and put them on the radiator. As the discomfort that comes from the warming of toes and fingers began to pulse in my hands and feet, I smelled the warming wool. The physical pain of toes and fingers rolled into the drying mittens on the radiator. It is now a reminder of a sorrowful childhood.

As we keep our eyes and hearts on the journey to where we are heading, to home, we look now at our actual inner noises.

NAMING YOUR INTERIOR NOISES

Look at the partial list below. What weighs you down on your way to the *Still*?

guilt   good intentions   life changes   nagging voices   apathy   fear   negative self-talk   memories   un-forgiveness   weight/diet envy   anger   bad habits   raising kids   drugs   learned powerlessness   anxiety   hate grief/sadness   unreal expectations   demands   cynicism   fear of silence   deep wounds   tragedy   Christmas   secondhand relationships   childhood scripts   self-image   greed

—pause & reflect—

Make this list yours. Circle, cross out, and add.
What keeps me from being still in my heart?
How invested am I in this noise?
How long and loud has it been around?
As you identify one of these, do a little tracking. How does your definition for noise help your identification?
Where and when does this weighted noise appear?

This information won't stop our noises. We can, however, find comfort in walking together. We are all plagued by obstructions to finding the stillness we are looking for. Each of us is in a different place on our journey, each with our share of what we are sorry for, what we wish we could change, or what we believe was done to us by another.

Let me reassure you. There is nothing on the list above that can keep you from the *Still* and the peace dwelling there. Surely you know that.

"I am sorry for my sin." David the Psalmist 38:17–20

"Forgive one another, quickly and thoroughly . . ." the apostle Paul teaches in Eph. 4:32

"I'll make a clean breast of my failures to God." David the Psalmist 32:5

"I forgive your sin. Get up. Take your stretcher and start walking," Jesus says in Mark 2:9

The noise recedes as the healing, forgiving, waiting on, and letting go of the voices sinks slowly and becomes the background of life. The freedom of the *Still* moves into the spaces they leave behind. This is the depth of life and the self being created even today in this moment. The *Still* is within us.

We are free to enter in. There is not a noise in our world that changes who you are in Christ Jesus. It's the weight of carrying that noise that slows down our journey. We've been dragging some of this junk around for a lifetime. And the stoppage disappears as we regret and acknowledge that it has happened. In that nanosecond as we ask for help, the noise recedes. We let it go.

"God's son purges all our sin," the disciple John discovers and writes in I John 1:7

You and I have yearned for a place, a home where the dirt doesn't matter and we can find rest from struggling with the conflict and melee inside us. You are more than the noises in your life. *The Still* embraces you as you are. We don't enter already healed and healthy. That's where we are going. Let's go find the best part of who we are!

We are headed home. There is healing here, and joy, forgiveness, and satisfaction.

A CALL TO COME AWAY AND WALK FOR A MOMENT

Breathe in . . .

Breathe out . . .

See, the door to the *Still* is before you.

As you reach for the doorknob, you hesitate and you are stopped.

Something stands in your way.

Noises are busting in . . . Is it worry? Leftover anger? Is it a familiar and unwanted voice?

Put a name to the noise(s)._____.

Slow way down.

Breathe in . . .

Breathe out . . .

You find yourself standing before a table laden with odd-sized boxes, tissue paper, tape, a marker, and labels.

In this moment, take each noise that stands in your way, pick them up, one by one.

Using the tissue paper, wrap them carefully.

Now, find a box that fits. Place each noise gently in a box and tape it shut several times, making sure it's tight.

Breathe in . . .

Breathe out . . .

Now, pick up the marker and labels and write a name on each box.

Take your time: each needs gentle care. They have been with you a long time.

Breathe in . . .

Breathe out . . .

In your mind think of someplace to deposit them, safe

THE ART OF LIVING DEEPLY

and secure—your attic, basement, garage, the trunk of your car.

Do what you need to do to get the boxes to this depository.

Open the door, push them in, far to the back, in the dark, out of reach.

Close the door, lock it.

Step away.

Walk away.

Breathe in . . .

Breathe out.

The *Still* awaits.

THE SURROUNDING STILLNESS

Streaks of lightning pierced the shadows on the wall, breaking my sleep. The wind whistling in through the bathroom vent roused my curiosity, but it was the crashing thunder at four AM that finally got me out of bed and on my feet. Grabbing my robe, I stepped out onto the balcony for a front-row seat.

The sky was rolling with clouds, and wind was moving the tops of the trees. Flashes of distant lightning lit the air, the tree line, the yard.

As spectacular as this storm was, it was the delicate melody coming out of the night between thunder claps, a solitary song rising from the darkness, that launched me into an unforgettable event. The turbulence exploding around me faded away as this delicate strain from a small bird captured me and spoke louder, inviting me to follow.

Music in the middle of nature's madness? A songbird expresses to me the mystery and wonder of the *Still*.

"Silence is the music of another world," said Pico Iyer.

Another world . . .

To enter that other world, we follow the bend on the path less traveled. We steer our steps to forge a new relationship with noise. There is no absence of noise or turning it off successfully. We won't attempt to spend our time here to learn new methods, but instead to unlearn some of what we already know. Our old reactions to noise slip away as we respond to the moment at hand. The journey includes increasing our ability to listen to our inner companion, the ability to hear new melodies and messages in the world around us. Our place of clarity of sound and the voice of God awaits, in a place that lies within us—what I have come to call the *Still*.

Another world . . .

Consider that songbird in the midst of chaos. She sings whether she is in a tree or sitting on a fence post in the middle of a field of daisies. She is created to sing. Now think about us in this chaotic world, the one driven by desires, contradictions, and insane voices. Like the warbler we are created to live in a space apart, as it were, where the notes inside us come forth simply, unhurried, rhythmic, and full.

Once we find our way to the sacred *Still*, we can be solidly grounded in who we truly are everywhere, all the time, in every circumstance.

SURROUNDED BY NOISE

The image of a small bird in the midst of a storm doing what she was created to do can be viewed from several perspectives. We might hear her being drowned out by the storm that swirls around her, or we may hear her melody alive and well with the storm fading, in which case the noise of the storm becomes an accompaniment of sorts, adding a harmony line.

> If a wren can cling to a spray a-swing
>
> In a mad May wind, and sing and sing,
>
> As if she'd burst for joy, why cannot I
>
> Contented lie in HIS quiet arms,
>
> Beneath His sky, unmoved by earth's annoy?
>
> —Robert Haven Schauffler

It took me a while with some help from a friend to recognize that the difference in what we perceive is a matter of focus. What rises to the forefront of our mind is either the stillness surrounding and within us or the noise in our life. This is so because, given our limited energy and capacity to perceive, we can focus only on one central thing at a time.

Here's the truth.

Every noise *is* surrounded by silence.

We don't have to manufacture our own stillness. It exists all around us. We are encircled by silence first. Sound comes out of silence. For most of us, noise fills the forefront of our lives because that is what we focus on. But our movement into the *Still* is a journey to find the silence around the noise, paying special attention to what exists between noises. We allow the noise to sink into the background and the stillness to come out of the shadows, move in, and be a part of the present.

Inner or outer noise—it doesn't matter. The sea of silence surrounding it is what we seek.

If we try to turn off or drown out the noise, we are wasting our limited energy on never-ending busy work. If we shutter the noise and focus on what we desire, such as stillness, quiet, calm, and serenity, we grow into finding the stillness around us. The sea of silence originates in and through God.

In that swirling storm the tiny bird sang her song, and by chance I focused on her. And because of that, I was free to find joy in the moment.

What we want, what this journey is all about, is not to stop the noise. It is to gain a sense of God's presence in the midst of life's busyness, chaos, and storms and to grow in our ability to hear and clarify God's voice.

—*pause & reflect*—

When have you heard music in the middle of a storm?

Where do you focus, on storms or silence?

Where is your focus in this moment?

UNLEARNING

Would we have joined together on this journey if we hadn't admitted to ourselves that we needed answers? And as good students, we are seeking more. At this point our journey takes an interesting U-turn.

What was once the central theme of our lives, noise, is turning on its heels. There was a time when we had been swept up into following our head and the habits it had formed. We had learned to react to noise instantaneously by embracing it or attempting to stop it any way we could. But our focus is changing. Our path now is following the silence. As we make our way to the *Still*, we let go of the noises in our life to unlearn that with which we are familiar.

The time has come to put our hearts first.

On my journey there came a time when I recognized that I had slowly and subtly become quieter inside. I share with you here briefly a few ways I've been unlearning these past years.

I relate this to you now, with laughter and a smile. When I study something I truly love, I can get very prideful and perfectionistic. As a good student, I want to get it right. So I was seriously considering journeying toward a more contemplative faith-life, and I wanted to do it the right way. I read books, attended retreats, listened attentively, and pursued a degree to become a Spiritual Director.

As a result, I had the privilege of walking with great teachers who had found a way, their way to journey. I attempted to follow precisely what I had been taught.

It took a three-month-old puppy named Pikku-Ilo, Finnish for "little delight," to end my attempt at perfection. Early one morning, this bundle of wiggling delight hopped onto my lap. I began scolding him for interrupting my quiet time when one of those never-to-be-forgotten moments occurred. As I pushed him away from me, I realized he was life itself unfolding in front of me, and I was foolishly shutting down the sweet reality of that moment.

That event forever dispelled my illusion of having to walk to the *Still* in anyone else's shoes. I released myself from getting too serious about my journey and being locked into doing it the expert's way. I began my own journey to the *Still* for real as I ran my fingers through the soft, golden puppy fur.

I was to realize much later that the simple beauty of that moment was the freedom I had been given. I had found the very mystery of living in the present, and that is what my teachers had been guiding me toward, each in their own way. I never refused that soft furry guy again. He became a reminder of life in the moment, a reality check of my focus and receptivity.

"Enlightenment is not so much knowing as unknowing; it is not so much learning as unlearning." Richard Rohr

My unlearning continued.

For all sorts of reasons, "L.P. Korte"—Let's Plan Korte—became one of my nicknames. I developed a plan for everything. Sad to say I would go on our yearly vacations already planning for the next year. I built the fun vacation in my head and heart, the ideal trip! And when we were actually in the car heading toward the cabin in Wisconsin, I was building the trip for next year. The ideal destroyed the actual. I traded in the real to have the imagined. Living in the future gave me tunnel vision. I existed for the future, always believing things would be better. I envisioned what we'd do next month, next week, and tomorrow. I was stuck looking past the moments available. Since childhood, I had been telling myself that life would get better. And I continued living in that. Next year we would have more money, more time, a better car, and the kids would be older and easier to travel with.

I think of those years now as lost years, out-of-touch years. The saddest part is those closest to me missed *who I was* and I missed *who they were* in so many little ways. Those well-planned happenings never lived up to my expectations. Many precious moments went unfulfilled for the need to control my life. The unlearning came slowly, bit by bit, as I grew in focusing on this moment and releasing living in the future. Somewhere along the way I planted my feet on solid ground.

"God loves the earthy." Hildegard of Bingen

I love being with books and thoughts. I remember the books, the libraries, and the hours I've spent studying and researching. My unlearning took a great stride forward as I began to understand the placement of my lifelong love of books and study. I was willing to be changed from the inside out. I knew it would be hard. I sadly began to think that because this absorbing love of mine took up so much of my time, I would have to let it go.

The U-turn came as I made a discovery. I had always been a good student for my parents, my teachers, and my bosses over the years. I had been taught to give my new-found knowledge away. As I made this turn, I began to understand that my studies reveal to me many insights meant just for me. As I unlearned who the recipient of these new understandings was to be—me—I found I was freed to enter the mystery of just being myself.

The unlearning was complete as I accepted reassurance that the continuing times of insight would become a means of walking and talking with God. Those times along the way are not meant for a world out there but for the world in here.

"Incubate the divine life . . . grow God organically in our own life." Sue Monk Kidd

— pause & reflect —

Do you consider yourself a good student?

Good or bad student, how does that change the way you let go to unlearn?

Do you ever ponder a new insight?

Do you have a need to share with someone? Who?

How much time do you spend in the past? The future?

When was the last time you let the awareness of a quiet moment inform a decision?

SLOW DOWN

We get it . . . But still we need to get there on time!

We get it, we need to get from here to there, from home to work. We're running a little late, so we push it. There are, after all, consequences at home, at school, and at work for not being on time.

Is there ever a time to slow down?

When you're going to visit a friend, are you in a hurry?

When traveling to visit this friend, how does this trip differ from going to work? Does the pace you set change, how?

Where and for whom do you rush?

When we're entering an interstate highway, such as I-66 flowing west out of Washington D.C., where we live, it is understood that we must yield as we merge with the flow of traffic. That flow, whether fast or slow, directs our speed. Imagine for a moment that we enter the on-ramp to a packed four- or five-lane highway, but on this day there is no flow to merge into because the road is empty. It is totally clear of cars and trucks. We are the only vehicle in sight.

How fast would we go?

My honest response would be, "Step on the gas. It's free time for me!"

Most of us react to the familiar sights and sounds of hurry by doing just that, speeding up. Our rush to get there, wherever "there" is, is our immediate reaction. We are focused out there somewhere. Unlearning involves slowing down our pace and responding in an even manner. It's time to set our motor on cruise control and truly notice what we have been whizzing by every day. Slowing down allows us to apply a solid response to noise.

It is to the *Still* we are walking. How we move through our day affects our movement toward that desire.

"To affect the quality of the day, that is the highest of arts."
Henry David Thoreau

—pause & reflect—

Do you consider yourself a person in a hurry?
How often are you in a rush?

If you had the roads to yourself,
how fast would you travel?

On the path to the *Still*, how do you
envision yourself walking? At what pace?

I am often in a hurry. I thought I was wired that way. But I had to find a way to slow down. My way may seem a bit odd, but is gets me to where I want to go with softer steps. There are moments when my body and my mind are racing. I physically stop in my tracks and tell myself to slow down. I slowly put one foot in front of the other, purposing to walk across the room almost in slow motion. I stroll across the room thinking "What's the hurry?"

Let go of the rush. Unlearning our reactions to noise, for rush is noise, too, and then replacing them with our individual ways to respond is part of this journey. Engaging our physical bodies and our overactive minds in a slow, solid response takes precedence on this path.

COACHING HELP

For practice, purpose pacing yourself. Try this in the grocery store next time you're there. Slow down and actually engage in walking slower up and down the aisles, observing more than what you have come for. Leave the eggs and the milk in the refrigerator section for an extra five minutes. You will be surprised and delighted. It will make your day!

LISTENING

The sounds of noise begin to fade as the volume of silence increases. We turn to our individual receptive natures. Our personal listening abilities move front and center. Unlearning teaches us to let go of what we know and to move forward, poised to discover the simple music of the *Still*.

My husband and I spent many years learning to communicate in our relationship and then, in turn, taught other couples. By far, the toughest skill to teach and then validate that it actually took effect is *listening*. At a glance it appears easy, and most individuals will say they are good at it. (I won't spend time here refreshing your memory on what it takes to be a good listener. The "Helps" section below contains the five skills of listening that we found most beneficial.) This life discipline stands apart as most important in the *Still,* where we do less talking and where listening is primary. As I taught it, this is by no means passive listening. We discovered, as others did, that listening is an active sport. It requires the sharpening of communication skills.

Here is the essence of what my husband and I had to learn and then teach others. We listen beyond the words that are spoken. As we find understanding, we ask ourselves, "What isn't being spoken here?" We enter into the other's words, and body language. We let go of ourselves and put our own answers, our ideas, and our judgments on hold to hear clearly what the other speaks. This skill is precious. Listening opens the door to the sounds of silence, the presence of God and the voice that speaks within us from beyond the silence.

Understand that deep listening is a process of creating, healing, and maturing. It is a challenging process demanding honesty and patience. Time is required for growth. We soon discover that restraint of our vocal cords is necessary to hear this new voice coming out of stillness. Listening does not require many words.

"My greatest weapon is mute prayer." Mohandas Gandhi

Our relationship with noise is making that U-turn mentioned earlier. Noise is a given. It's no longer an adversary. No need to spend energy ignoring it or trying to stomp it out. In fact, it has at times an uncanny way of telling us the truth. Noises can become valuable assets in the growing, changing life we are moving into. That distraction that keeps you from the *Still* may hold within it a gem. It may just be the center of your conversation with the Lord that day.

"While doing centering prayer, the practice is to let go of any thought or perception. The priority is to be silent as possible and when that is not possible to let the noises or the thoughts be the *sacred symbol* for a while, without analyzing them." Thomas Keating

—*pause & reflect*—

"You never listen." Is this a familiar charge by friends?

Are you a good listener?
Or is talking your preferred communicating style?

What persistent thought has distracted you recently?

SOUNDS OF SILENCE

The sounds of silence wait for us to follow. The music created ushers us into the *Still*. With each melody we follow, the notes reach out to all of our God-given senses, from smelling to touching to tasting to hearing and to seeing. In all our being, we are created to receive each new song.

After the U-turns we have made we are on our way with each new awareness that emerges we find that something different exists. We can no longer define our journey to the *Still* in terms of steps. There are no steps, for these melodies come in waves. They won't be captured, just experienced. We hold them for a moment and then release. We enter into an event in time and space to be remembered in that way. It will not happen just that way again.

We continue moving forward, for no strain of melody remains the same. This is a personal storyline written only within ourselves. Because of this, we allow a wide margin for failure. Our expectations change, and we learn to meet stillness in seconds at first, and then slowly slide into minutes.

We don't have to find God in the silence. *God has already found us.*

The silence is a deepening of the present.

Awakening to the silence surrounding us is a lifetime of simple, profound events. What follows below are events of silence that have ushered others into the *Still*.

The soft fur of a puppy between your fingers early in the morning.

The creaks and groans of your house at midnight.

The smell of grass after a spring rainfall.

That first sip of coffee in the morning.

Viewing the devastation of your neighborhood after a tornado touch down.

Closing the office door on Friday night after a devastating week.

Holding the hand of a friend as they grieve over the death of their child.

In the noonday sun, snow slowly sliding off the roof.

Holding your child in the wee hours of the morning.

— *pause & reflect* —

What is the stillness around you?

When have you experienced it?

What does it look like? Sound like?
Feel like? Taste like? Smell like?

A few weeks ago, my husband and I were having a discussion about something I barely remember from the local news. We were grumpy, answering each other with irritated voices. We spoke from a position of being right and expanded the discussion to areas we knew we did not agree on. Our discussion gained steam and got louder. I left the room to start breakfast, but I couldn't get that noise out of my head. I continued the argument in my head, adding my points. The noise of hurt and not being heard resonated within me. The rest of the morning we worked alone, each on our own projects, keeping our comments to ourselves. By noon I realized my inner peace and the space between my husband and me was contracted, disconnected. I felt alone, as if a dark cloud covered my inner landscape. As the awareness came, I questioned myself. "What am I doing here in this unpleasant space?" I had another option, and I decided to sit in the *Still*, the presence of God. Since God often speaks to me through nature, I took a seat on the couch with my legs up and looked out the sliding glass door below onto the grassy area with palm trees, a small pond, and lush bushes. I took several deep breaths to quiet the noise and focus. I sensed my entering into the stillness and connection with God. What took me so long? As I sat there for some time observing the quiet scene, two white heads, side by side, appeared from behind one of the bushes. As if on cue, they stepped fuller into view and lifted their beautiful white underbellies edged in brown; then they took flight, soaring directly at the glass door. With ease they continued their flight past my sight and up and over the roof. I had never seen an egret fly before. Overwhelmed, I sat there for a long time. A shift occurred in that time and space—inner spaciousness opened, gratefulness softened my heart, and love flooded my spirit. Revisiting my conversation from earlier in the morning, I was able to reconnect with my husband. I no longer felt closed in with resentment and anger but was open and able to share in love. A fluid, open, nourishing space of reconnection with the Presence, me, and my husband was created. I realized that my own noise disrupts the peace between us. We deserve my taking time to pause and enter the eye of the hurricane where I find the *Still*. —Cindi Bell

Entering into the still

Although my mind is racing

And the calendar is full

My soul yearns for quiet

Even for a few minutes

To notice God

Silence means listen.

If I am in a garden

I stop and marvel at the intricacy

And detail of a flower

Who can make such a beauty or variety?

If I am at the lake

I listen to the rhythmic waves

And am reminded of Christ

Being my living water

On a summer day I look at the sky

Amazed at the wonder of the blueness

The wispy clouds wafting by

> Or the brilliant oranges and reds at sunrise
>
> Or the starry host at night
>
> How big is God?
>
> Taste and see and hear and feel and smell
>
> The God of creation
>
> Take God in
>
> Notice God's world
>
> God is near
>
> God is here. —Kathy Kelly

HELPS

We find as we become aware of our personal listening habits, that it's not about you, it's about becoming intensely aware of what's around you. And the key to being a good listener is to follow not to lead.

The five skills of listening, adapted from *Alive and Aware: Improving Communications in Relationships* by Sherod Miller, Elam W. Nunnally, and Daniel B. Wackman:

Attend: Pay full attention with your senses, body, and mind. Stop other activity that may be distracting.

Acknowledge: Respond, showing interest respectfully, allowing yourself the energy of that sound to move you. Enter into that energy.

Invite: After a pause, encourage through thoughts or words more, drawing out the sight or sound of silence.

Summarize: Repeat, jot down, or accept the sound as silence speaking.

Ask: Finally, don't hesitate to clarify what you have heard. It is a powerful way to connect with the world around us through silence.

A CALL TO COME AWAY AND WALK FOR A MOMENT

Breathe in . . .

Breathe out.

Silence.

You take a step forward.

You breathe in a familiar fragrance, one you've smelled before.

A smile spreads on your face.

The fragrance brings with it a sweet taste—perhaps your Grandmother's oatmeal cookies.

Breathe in . . .

Breathe out . . .

It's slow-down time.

You see so clearly now what is in front of you.

No need to hurry.

You're here.

You have arrived at Peace.

Thank you, Lord.

GETTING LOST ONCE AGAIN

We were on the right track.

It was making sense. We found stillness.

We had it!

So, where did it go?

After winding our way through the maze of noise in which we live, and after entering into experiencing moments in the *Still*—which is always the direction of our journey—we wake up one morning bewildered. Maybe even lost.

How could we forget the way?

LOST

Getting lost on the way to the *Still* that first time comes as a surprise. Losing the way can be viewed as a disorienting nuisance or as a valuable asset to the journey.

Our lives are filled with details and obligations, old and new relationships, great joys and deep sorrows. Every item on our list insists on our attention, bringing new drama with mystery and intrigue to our doorstep. We don't plan, in fact, we can't plan for the unexpected. Was it days or over weeks that we found ourselves slipping into old habits. Or did we simply abandon the journey we were on? Can we reclaim the path? Do we really want to?

This is how I got lost again recently.

One morning, emerging from a vile stomach flu, my head in a haze of illness and my body screaming and feeling ripped open and violated, I opened my eyes and groped around for sights and sounds of silence. I fully expected to pick up where I had left off in my journey into stillness from the past week. I began by trying my normal form of deep breathing.

It was gone, and no amount of sucking in and blowing out was going to reawaken the calm.

As the days continued and I moved further away from the illness, the restlessness, the lack of spiritual energy, and the focus that I had taken for granted had vanished. It was as if knowing the way I had faded and disappeared. What had held life itself for me, what had held the here and now and the essence of me, what had been an open door to keeping company with God—all of it was out of sight.

I've lost it, I thought, dismayed.

I kept going over the past, asking where did I go wrong? What step did I miss? I tried hard to recreate from memory how I'd done it.

I whined, "Do I have to go all the way back there?" I hope no one else heard that self-serving rant, because I didn't like what was coming out of my head. I began to rerun the journey to the *Still* in my heart.

THE MOMENT

As I did this, I was reminded that this moment, the one I was currently in, it was the key to walking to the *Still*. There are no keyed-in patterns, no ladder rungs to count off to find our way. We don't know what lies ahead until it unfolds. We are to live in the moment we have. It is risky, and we rely on what we have in the here and now.

If we have moved toward the *Still* holding the belief that we climb a ladder to God or if we have taken the journey to the *Still* as a problem to be solved, we'll have missed the depth of the *Still*.

God descends any ladders we may have set up for ourselves. God comes to us. There is no way we can practice enough, study enough, or get it right enough. Jesus's feet on the ground, his death on that tree, and living life again is how we manage to know the way to the *Still*. It was done for us. We follow his steps directly into resurrection. Our lives are destined for eternity.

There is no final arrival in the *Still*. There are no graduations, no perfect scores or diplomas. We never become experts. We don't formalize our path. And there is no need for "I got it," because we are having it. We are in the moment, on the move, and a step backward doesn't exist. Losing our way is part of the way.

Being lost is part of moving in the *Still*. It doesn't bring death on this journey; quite the opposite, it brings deeper life. We are learning to live in contradiction. It's all good. There's life and then there's life.

Eager to move on, we travel lighter, emptied of the unnecessary load of getting it right and reaching a goal. The child within us heals little by little as we let go. And as we feel a new liberty to be who we are, we find an increasing freedom to know Jesus as more than a familiar Bible figure.

RESURRECTION

In our faith, we call it resurrection. Finding ourselves helpless, up the creek without a paddle, letting go to the movement of life within us, releasing our breath, being present to the sounds of silence—all this revives our life, and we are still once more. Resurrection is the background music of the *Still*.

Sunrise, sunset, sunrise—these are the signs of resurrection every day in our life. It is all around us. The dance of the earth has resurrection written all over it. Opening, setting, opening again is the beat of living life, but different every full day. Never are there two showings the same. Year by year, season by season, the syncopation goes on. Life to death to life always on the move, never two seasonal months the same. We are intrinsically a part of this major melody, light and dark, heat and ice.

And that dead grass in our front yards . . . we look at it in January and by April resurrection has occurred. That which we thought dead has come back to life. Resurrection is the natural movement for life. Jesus came to earth to show us his way. We were meant to be "children of the living God." (Matthew 22:28)

THE INVITATION REMAINS

The invitation to the *Still* remains, and our assurance of its existence lies deep within us. We know we are already united with God. We can't get lost, because our life force, Christ, lives within us. In his words, "I will not leave you lost and desolate because I live, you will live also. I am in my Father, you in me, and I in you." (John 14:18)

The *Still* lives within us. It always has.

The *Still*, the rest, the silence of God dwells in the core of our being. Jesus said it this way: "Those who love me will keep my word and my father will love them and we will come to them and make our home with them." (John 14:23)

The Spirit of the Lord dwells in us.

The Apostle Paul shared this with the Christian community following the Resurrection of Jesus: "If the spirit of him who raised Jesus from the dead dwells in you, he who raised Christ Jesus from the dead will give life to your mortal bodies also through his spirit which dwells in you." (Romans 8:11)

The fullness of God the Father, Son, and Holy Spirit resides in us, and is at home in us.

"God dwells deeply within us, and his love becomes complete in us." (1 John 4:11–12)

God lives within us, God's love is complete and our love is complete as we reside in God.

Then I remembered some wise advice given to me by a person who had gone before me, a man named Tommy Tyson, founder of a retreat center in North Carolina.

"When you find yourself dressed in graduation robes, turn around and you'll find yourself in swaddling clothes once again."

THE GRADUATION ROBES

I didn't think I had graduated, but I had become very familiar and well-schooled in my way to enter into the *Still*. It was well practiced, and I ticked my way off in my head: up early in the morning.; fix coffee; sit in darkness; deep breaths; enter in; dog jumps on lap for a pet; after time switch on light; read quietly; pause; reflect. Easy peasy!

Diminished focus and the jarring energy that comes from noise are what waylay us. Noise becomes seductively demanding. Distractions and emergencies, illness, personal loss, some great and wonderful experiences all make up our lifetime. A full life brings it all together at one time.

A graduation suggests we've completed a grade, a course of study, and are leaving something behind to find something more. We've accomplished a goal for ourselves or our parents. Most of us spent a year in kindergarten, and this achievement gave us access to first grade. And so it's gone over our lifetime: Achievement equals success equals rewards. So we try in whatever we choose to do to climb the ladder of what we view as success. Walking to the *Still* comes into play here. We are going toward something we want, a time of stillness and calm in a hectic world.

The disciples were taught this very thing by Jesus. "He that would save his life will lose it." Self-help and determining our own way will only get us so far in the journey. It's losing your step and following the one who knows where we are going that is the way to the *Still*.

THE SWADDLING CLOTHES

A graduation doesn't take very long as milestones go in our lives. It's usually just a ceremony where we get patted on the back for doing a good job. Walking past that moment, stepping back to start again, is a thankless and rudimental choice to make as we journey.

We may get helplessly lost and then turn to find ourselves in swaddling clothes, fearful, tired, and frustrated. Is this the path for us?

Have you been around an infant recently? The "swaddling clothes" of our culture are called onesies, a single piece of attire that slips over the baby's head. The arms are positioned in the holes and the entire garment is fastened by two snaps between the legs. That's a huge difference from the concept of swaddling clothes. These ancient garments may have felt like an embrace, but they were meant primarily for restricting movement. The wrap did provide a sense of protection and calm, a sense of love and warmth.

When we get lost, we are in the throes of flailing, wandering, and wondering, often combined with anger and resignation. Swaddling clothes metaphorically limit our darkness but reset our walk to the *Still*. As we continue our journey, a change begins to occur. As we once again find and live in the moment, we find freedom inside our slowly evolving resurrection.

Once free from undue tension caused by being out of step, the simple responses that a child accepts emerge. We have more clarity and volume to the sounds of silence. Eager to move on, we travel lighter, emptied of the unnecessary load we've been carrying around.

The child within us is healing through letting go and accepting the freedom to be who we are created to be. The freedom extended finds Jesus as more than an important figure in scripture.

We are the children of the resurrection. (Luke 20:36)

We are united in resurrection with Christ. (Romans 6:5)

When we believe we have lost our way, are we ever lost? Not really.

We don't get lost; we get repurposed. We begin again for the first time. Unlearning has found its way again to the forefront of our journey. We don't get the expected applause for finding our way to the *Still*. We choose to enter into the loss of losing our way and gain a much deeper path.

The assurance is all around us. The sunrise is preceded by darkness and often with faint color. As it begins to rise, the new light of the day keeps moving toward a palette of color, a full range of tones and timbres. The sounds of silence are almost deafening at times!

Like a beginning artist seeing the details of a sunset for the first time or a musician discovering the quiet melody locked away in the deafening noise of the brass, the *Still* has been there all the time. The dwelling place of God is quietly tucked away in you.

HELPS

If you get lost—and you will—here are a few things to keep in mind.

Don't wallow in where you've been.

Step into this moment as soon as you are able.

You now have a new lens, a fresh canvas, a deepening melody.

Welcome home and enter in once again.

A CALL TO COME AWAY AND WALK...FOR A MOMENT...

So the breathing isn't working . . .

There is no prescribed way to get unlost . . .

Take a breath . . .

Be here . . .

Don't know your way?

That's okay . . .

Let go . . .

Can you see the doorway across the space?

Take a small baby step . . .

One step at a time . . .

The *Still* awaits your presence . . .

THE JOURNEY'S END IS REALLY A NEW BEGINNING

Because we're stopping in the here and now, we are not really ending. We are continuing our steps forward to the *Still*.

Never ending, always leaning forward is the daily walk. Moving, loving, seeing with more clarity is the way of the *Still*.

Thomas Merton has a distinct way of saying what I have been saying throughout these pages.

"When your tongue is silent, you can rest in the silence of the forest. When your imagination is silent, the forest speaks to you . . . But when your mind is silent, then the forest suddenly becomes magnificently real and blazes transparently with the reality of God." Daily Meditations from His Journal, March 17, 1952, II. 470–71.

DR. TINA KORTE

Certified Spiritual Director (CERT S.D.), Benedictine Monastery, Duluth, MN; D. Min., M.Div., Luther Seminary, St. Paul MN; M.A., M.S., College of St. Thomas of Villanova, Miami, Fl.

A recent arrival to Northern Virginia from the Midwest, Tina brings to her new home in Northern Virginia, the gifts and experience of counselor, spiritual director and retreat provider.

In her 35 years as a therapist, Tina has walked with and listened to others. She has entered into a still and contemplative place in her life. As a spiritual guide, she feels a need to give to others, time and opportunity to identify their deeper living possibilities, the ones they have been given. She uses a creative and unique approach as she joins you on your walk.

Tina, co-authored, with her husband *The Marriage-Go-Round*, (Bethany House Publishers, 1991) and *Men and Women; Building Communication*, (Augsburg Fortress, 1995).

While writing and consulting for Prison Fellowship she developed an in-prison marriage retreat, including spouses, *Planted by the Living Waters; Growing as a Couple in Jesus Christ*, (Prison Fellowship, 1990).

Made in the USA
Columbia, SC
05 January 2018